*A*lways *Believe in Yourself and Your Dreams*

Copyright © 1997 by Stephen Schutz and Susan Polis Schutz.
Copyright © 1997 by Blue Mountain Arts, Inc.

All rights reserved. No part of this book may be reproduced in any
manner whatsoever without written permission from the publisher.

Library of Congress Catalog Card Number: 97-9937
ISBN: 0-88396-448-1

ACKNOWLEDGMENTS appear on page 48.

N design on book cover is registered in the U.S. Patent and Trademark
Office.

Manufactured in the United States of America
First Printing: April, 1997

♲ This book is printed on recycled paper.

Library of Congress Cataloging-in-Publication Data

Always believe in yourself and your dreams : a collection of poems /
    edited by Patricia Wayant.
        p. cm.
    ISBN 0-88396-448-1 (alk. paper)
    1. Self-actualization (Psychology)—Poetry. 2. American
    poetry—20th century. 3. Success—Poetry.
    I. Wayant, Patricia, 1953-   .
    PS595.S45A49 1997
    811.008'0353—DC21   97-9937
                                                            CIP

Blue Mountain Press ®

P.O. Box 4549, Boulder, Colorado 80306

*A*lways Believe
in Yourself
and Your Dreams

A collection of poems
Edited by Patricia Wayant

Don't Ever Doubt Yourself

You have so much to offer,
so much to give, and so much
you deserve to receive in return.
Don't ever doubt that.
Know yourself and all of your fine
    qualities.
Rejoice in all your marvelous strengths
    of mind and body.
Be glad for the virtues that are yours,
    and pat yourself on the back for all
    your many admirable achievements.

Keep positive.
Concentrate on that which
    makes you happy,
        and build yourself up.
Stay nimble of heart,
    happy of thought,
    healthy of mind, and
        well in being.

— Janet A. Sullivan

Your Life Holds
Unlimited Potential

You have the ability
to attain whatever you seek;
within you is every potential
you can imagine.
    Always aim higher than
you believe you can reach.
So often, you'll discover
that when your talents
are set free
by your imagination,
you can achieve any goal.
If people offer
their help or wisdom
as you go through life,
accept it gratefully.
You can learn much from those
who have gone before you.

Never be afraid or hesitant
to step off the accepted path
and head in your own direction
if your heart tells you
that it's the right way for you.
Always believe that you will
ultimately succeed
at whatever you do,
and never forget the value
of persistence, discipline,
and determination.
You are meant to be
whatever you dream
of becoming.

— Edmund O'Neill

You Deserve
a Life of Happiness

You will get only what you seek
You must choose your goals carefully
Know what you like
and what you do not like
Be critical about what you can do well
and what you cannot do well
Choose a career or lifestyle
    that interests you
and work hard to make it a success
Enter a relationship that is worthy of
everything that you are
physically and mentally capable of
Be honest with people
    help them if you can
but don't depend on anyone
    to make life easy
or happy for you
Only you can do that for yourself
Strive to achieve all that you like
Find happiness in everything you do
Love with your entire being
Love with an uninhibited soul
Make a triumph
of every aspect
of your life

— Susan Polis Schutz

Twelve Ways to Keep Smiling!

*H*old on to your dreams, and
never let them go ⇐ Show the rest
of the world how wonderful you are!
⇐ Give circumstances a chance, and
give others the benefit of the doubt
⇐ Wish on a star that shines in
your sky ⇐ Take on your problems
one by one and work things out ⇐
Rely on all the strength you have
inside ⇐ Let loose of the sparkle
and spirit that you sometimes try
to hide ⇐ Stay in touch with those
who touch your life with love ⇐
Look on the bright side and don't
let adversity keep you from winning
⇐ Be yourself, because you are filled
with special qualities that have
brought you this far, and that will
always see you through ⇐ Keep your
spirits up ⇐ Make your heart happy,
and let it reflect on everything you do!

— Douglas Pagels

The Power of Change
Is in Your Hands

Life is a set of circumstances that
you can change, improve,
and make better day by day.
It's your decision; it's in your hands.
Just like the potter at the wheel,
you are the force that turns and moves
the clay into a thing of beauty.
Like the painter's brush depicting
something fresh and new and picturesque,
you can create the scenery that's best
for you.

Each person has the power to take
control of every circumstance in life —
to change, improve,
and make it better day by day.
Not one of us can say:
"I must accept whatever comes my way,"
because the way we choose to go
through life is our decision.
The power of change is always
in your hands.

— Barbara J. Hall

Believe in Miracles!

Love your life.
Believe in your own power,
* your own potential,*
*   and your own innate goodness.*
Every morning, wake with the awe
* of just being alive.*
Each day, discover the magnificent,
* awesome beauty in the world.*
Explore and embrace life in yourself
* and in everyone you see each day.*
Reach within to find your own specialness.
Amaze yourself,
* and rouse those around you*
*   to the potential of each new day.*
Don't be afraid to admit
* that you are less than perfect;*
*   this is the essence of your humanity.*
Let those who love you help you.
Trust enough to be able to take.
Look with hope to the horizon of today,
* for today is all we truly have.*
Live this day well.
Let a little sunshine out as well as in.
Create your own rainbows.
Be open to all your possibilities;
* possibilities can be miracles.*
Always believe in miracles!

— Vickie M. Worsham

Let nothing hold you back from
exploring your wildest fantasies,
  wishes, and aspirations.
Don't be afraid to dream big
and to follow your dreams
  wherever they may lead you.
Open your eyes to their beauty;
open your mind to their magic;
open your heart to their possibilities.
Only by dreaming will you ever discover
who you are, what you want,
  and what you can do.
Don't be afraid to take risks,
  to become involved,
  to make a commitment.
Do whatever it takes to make
  your dreams come true.
Always believe in miracles,
  and always believe in you!

— Julie Anne Ford

Create Your Own World

*Every day has
its own rewards
and its own unique challenges.
None of us has
the same exact worries
or responsibilities,
because life is shaped
around each of us as individuals.
It's important to remember that
we all create our own worlds.
Who we are and the way we act
are how we control our lives.
There are endless opportunities
for us to change and rearrange
the day-to-day moments
   we are given.
It's up to each of us to decide
which way we want to go;
how far or how fast
we go in life are the choices
we all must make for ourselves.*

— Dena Dilaconi

It's Up to You

*This life is the only one
you're given.
Look for opportunities to grow,
and never be discouraged
in your efforts to do so.
Replace your weaknesses
with positives;
take life's broken pieces
and re-create your dreams.
Never measure the future
by the past;
let yesterday become a memory
and tomorrow a promise.*

*Begin each day by focusing
on all that is good,
and you'll be in a position
to handle whatever comes along.
Take responsibility for
your actions;
never make excuses
for not being the best
you can be.
If you should slip,
be comforted by the thought
that we all do at times.
Determine your tomorrow
by the choices you make today,
and you'll find yourself living
in joy and triumph.*

— Linda E. Knight

The Secret to Life
Is Living It
One Day at a Time

*O*ur lives are made up of a million
moments, spent in a million different ways.
Some are spent searching for love, peace, and
harmony. Others are spent surviving day to day.
But there is no greater moment than when we
find that life, with all its joys and sorrows, is
meant to be lived one day at a time.

It's in this knowledge that we discover the
most wonderful truth of all. Whether we live in
a forty-room mansion, surrounded by servants
and wealth, or find it a struggle to manage the
rent month to month, we have it within our
power to be fully satisfied and live a life with
true meaning.

One day at a time — we have that ability,
through cherishing each moment and rejoicing
in each dream. We can experience each day anew,
and with this fresh start we have what it takes
to make all of our dreams come true. Each day
is new, and living one day at a time enables us
to truly enjoy life and live it to the fullest.

— Regina Hill

Never Let Go of Hope

*One day
you will see
that it all
has finally come together.*

*What you have
always wished for
has finally come to be.*

*You will look back
and laugh at what has passed
and you will ask yourself,
"How did I get through all of that?"*

*Just
never let go of hope.
Just
never quit dreaming.
And
never let love
depart from your life.*

— jancarl campi

The Path to a Dream

The path to a dream is paved
  with sacrifices
and lined with determination.
And though it has many stumbling blocks
  along the way
and may go in more than one direction,
  it is marked with faith.
It is traveled by belief and courage,
  persistence and hard work.
It is conquered with a willingness
to face challenges and take chances,
  to fail and try again and again.
Along the way, you may have to confront
  doubts, setbacks, and unfairness.
But when the path comes to an end,
you will find that there is no greater joy
than making your dream come true.

— Barbara Cage

Just Be Yourself

To be who you are
is to be enough.
To share who you are
is to share enough.
To do what you love
is to do enough.

There is no race to win
and nothing to be proven,
only dreams to be nurtured,
a self to be expressed,
and love to be shared.

Never doubt your worth,
and always know,
without any doubt,
that you are truly valued.

— Donna Newman

Make the Most of Every Day, and Celebrate All That You Are

*L*ive by your own light ← Shine by your own star ← Do what you always wanted to do with your life ← Envision the gift that you are ← Climb up the hills of your hopes and dreams ← Take whatever steps you need to take ← You can't get to the top if you don't try, and it's a journey you should definitely make ←

Try to find more time in your life ← Do it just for you ← The people you love and care about will be rewarded with your happiness, too ← When the calendar is far too full ← Keep the days from flying by ← Remember your youth when time took forever ← Rediscover that child inside ←

*Spend part of every day just doing
something you'd like to do ⭠ Today
will never come again, and yesterday
is through ⭠ The secret (if you'd like
to know) to finding happiness ⭠ Is
knowing that it's all around and that
your life is blessed ⭠ By being in
this moment and living a day at a
time ⭠ You have access to every gift
that will make your sunlight shine ⭠
Brighten your world with friendships
and love and wishes on a star ⭠*

*Make the most of every day ⭠ And
celebrate all that you are.*

— Douglas Pagels

Never Let Go of the Dreams in Your Heart

Sometimes it seems that our dreams
Crumble in our hands.
We think that we have failed
And that all we tried
So hard to attain
Will now always stay
Slightly out of reach.

But one failure cannot
Crumble the dreams
That years of hard work
And dedication have built.
So hold on to your dreams.
Believe in yourself,
And you will find that a
Bright tomorrow
Waits just around the next turn.
You will make it.
You will be successful.
And your dream will come true...
Just keep believing!

— *Jennifer Eller*

Be Strong, and Don't Give Up

*Remember... there is a deeper strength
and an amazing abundance of peace
available to you.
Draw from this well;
call on your faith to uphold you.
Life continues around us,
even when our troubles seem to stop time.
There is always good in life.
Take a few minutes to distract yourself
from your concerns —
long enough to draw strength from a tree
or to find pleasure in a bird's song.
Return a smile;
realize that life is a series of levels,
cycles of ups and downs —
some easy, some challenging.
Through it all, we learn;
we grow strong in faith;
we mature in understanding.
The difficult times are often
the best teachers, and there is
good to be found in all situations.
Reach for the good.
Be strong, and don't give up.*

— Pamela Owens Renfro

To Get What You Want Out of Life...

*It takes believing in your dreams
and in what you know to be true.
Surviving disappointments
and the times when
   you're truly alone.
Awakening to see that you
   have made it through
the difficult times
with only yourself to depend on.
It takes facing the truth
that only you can shape your destiny.
Realizing that the footsteps
   you take today
are the ones that will
   lead you into tomorrow,
and they must be guided by
   an unswerving faith in yourself.
Understanding that the failures,
   setbacks, and hurts
life often gives us all
only serve as steppingstones
   to true happiness —
and if you follow the trail
instead of turning back,
only then will you recognize
   your strengths
and be able to view life
   from the summit.*

— Debra McCleary

Know Yourself

*Know what you can
and want to do in life
Set goals for yourself
and work hard to achieve them
Strive to have fun every day
Use your creativity as a means
of expressing your feelings
Be sensitive
in viewing the world
Develop a sense of confidence
Be honest with yourself
and with others
Follow your heart
and adhere to your own truths
Know that the more you give
the more you will receive
Believe in yourself
and your dreams
will come true*

— Susan Polis Schutz

Whatever you can do,
or dream you can... begin it.
Boldness has genius, power
and magic in it.

— *Goethe*

Nothing can bring you peace
but yourself.

— *Ralph Waldo Emerson*

Success Has No Limits...

There are no limits
to what you can do.
Your talents and abilities,
your uniqueness and warmth,
your strength and dedication
in everything you do —
all of these will help you
reach your dreams.

There are no limits
to what life has to offer you.
The world is full of possibilities,
just as you are filled with promise.
Seek, discover, and embrace with openness
the richness of experience.
Believe in yourself
and you will always know success.

— Michelle Richards

Let Your Heart
Show You the Way

Listen
    to the song in you.
It's there
in whatever puts stars
in your eyes
and makes your heart sing.
Listen
    to your feelings
and you will hear
who you are
and what you must do.
Listen
    to your needs
and you will know
where to find
what you are looking for.

Listen
to the wisdom within.
It is trying to lead you
to your destiny.
Listen
to the song in you
and your life
will be full of harmony.
You will be
who you were meant to be.
You will be complete
and at peace
and happier than you
have ever been —
if only you will
Listen
to the song in you.

—Nancye Sims

When You're Struggling
Over a Difficult Decision...

My best advice to you is to give it "the rocking chair test." Imagine that you're ninety years old, sitting on the porch and rocking in your chair as you reflect back on your life. Will you regret doing this — or <u>not</u> doing it? Pick the decision you can live with, and have no regrets in your choice. Believe in the choices you make.

— Anne Larnella Hood

A Creed for Being
the Best You Can Be

Speak and you will be heard;
make your words kind
and you will be judged so.
Love kindly and unselfishly,
with no wish to possess.
Search for who you are
and for what matters.
Give freely to all,
and you shall receive
so much more.
Listen to the troubles of others,
and your own shall be halved.
Live each day as your last,
treasuring each sight and sound.
Accept what you have
and all that is freely given.
Strive to be greater than
you were before.
Ask, and even your smallest wish
will be granted.
Dream of what can be —
a world of peace and beauty
for all to share.

— Stephanie Robinson

Trust in Yourself

I believe all of us have a built-in compass to help us get to wherever we desire to go. Don't forget to trust that compass, and refer to it often, for with that trusting will come the strength to bear whatever life deals you.

Don't get led astray. Ask your heart for the truth, and it will come up with the answer and the good judgment to make the decisions you'll need to make. Love everyone, and don't question love's reception. Do the best you can. Live each day as it comes. We can't get ahead of ourselves anyway.

Remember: just as you have questions now, somewhere inside you, and down the road, there will be better answers and workable solutions. It takes patience and trust to get through life's changes when you're trying to reach goals, solve problems, and make dreams come true. Though at times it may seem more than you can take, I know you are strong, and you can handle whatever comes your way. Trust in yourself.

— Donna Fargo

Only You Can Make the Right Things Happen in Your Life

You don't need anyone else
to give your life direction.
You know what's right for you.
Inside your heart exists
a special knowledge
of the plans you've made,
the hopes you have,
and the dreams you hold.
You may be hesitant at times,
even fearful to go on,
but that's a natural feeling
all of us go through.
What you need to remember
is what means the most to you
and how to keep alive your hopes
and dreams.
Then, with all the greatness
that is within you,
go in that new direction —
backed by your own faith,
decisive courage,
and a heart filled with dreams.
And remember that only you
can make the right things
happen in your life.

— Barbara J. Hall

Live Your Life
with Courage

Courage is admitting that you're afraid and facing that fear directly. It's being strong enough to ask for help and humble enough to accept it.

Courage is standing up for what you believe in without worrying about the opinions of others. It's following your own heart, living your own life, and settling for nothing less than the best for yourself.

Courage is daring to take a first step, a big leap, or a different path. It's attempting to do something that no one has done before, and all others thought impossible.

Courage is keeping heart in the face of disappointment, and looking at defeat not as an end but as a new beginning. It's believing that things will ultimately get better even as they get worse.

Courage is being responsible for your own actions, and admitting your own mistakes without placing blame on others. It's relying not on others for your success, but on your own skills and efforts.

Courage is refusing to quit even when you're intimidated by impossibility. It's choosing a goal, sticking with it, and finding solutions to the problems.

Courage is thinking big, aiming high, and shooting far. It's taking a dream and doing anything, risking everything, and stopping at nothing to make it a reality.

— Caroline Kent

Do Whatever You Need to Do...

If need be, go it alone —
your victory will be even sweeter.
If need be, go slowly —
how fast you get there
isn't important.
If need be, start over
*   again and again —*
success becomes closer each time.
If need be, accept whatever
*   you have to —*
it may not be easy to do,
but it makes everything easier.
If need be, stop running —
so that happiness can find you.
If need be, admit that
*   you need help —*
this is helping yourself.
If need be, ignore fear —
for without fear,
*   anything is possible.*
If need be, make a change —
it could change your life.
If need be, surrender —
without struggle, there is peace.
If need be, compromise —
but keep your principles.

If need be, continue
what seems to be impossible —
it only is impossible if you quit.
If need be, stop —
and a new life will start.
If need be, try something different —
you will be wiser.
If need be, wait —
amazing things happen every day.
If need be, live with uncertainty —
certainty is in trusting yourself.
If need be, have faith —
and faithfully you'll be given
strength.
If need be, go forward —
your dreams are waiting
patiently for you.

— Nancye Sims

There Is Only One
Key to Success:
Never Quit!

*Believe in yourself
and your vision of the future.
Surround yourself with
those who believe in you
and will help you achieve
your goals.
Keep your dream alive
despite the challenges
along the way.*

*There will always be those
who try to steal your dream
by laughter or criticism.
They cannot understand what
drives you to always want more.*

*In safety, there is no failure —
neither is there success.
Only by taking the risks
that others fear
can you achieve greatness.*

Change can be frightening,
but only by changing
can you experience growth.
Only by challenging yourself
to do what seems impossible
can you ever know how much
you can achieve.

There is only one key
to success:
never quit until you win.
It may require a lot of changing,
but you can do it.
The seed of greatness
lies within you.
Nurture it, and there
will be nothing you can't do.

— Lisa Marie Yost

You Can Design
Your Own Destiny

You are a wonderful person,
so do wonderful things.
You can make a difference
in your world.
You have a purpose;
you have the power;
you are magic.
You can create beauty,
recall the past,
plan the future.
You can soar in imagination.
You have the courage to question,
and you can choose to change.
The only limitations you have
are those in your own mind;
don't be satisfied with less than
all you can be.
Don't compare yourself with others;
draw your own dreams
and design your own destiny.
Live each day to the fullest.
Give a little more than you take.
Make this world a better place to live,
and always — always —
listen to your own heart,
for only you know what is best for you.

— Vickie M. Worsham

May There Never Be a Dream That Is Beyond Your Reach

May there be no dead ends in your life
and no roads traveled
  without blessings.
May no day be too short
  to fit love and laughter into it;
may time never be so scarce
  that you cannot give yourself
some quiet and gentle thoughts.
May there be no friends too busy for you
and no family member
  who doesn't greatly love you.

May there never be a dream
  beyond your reach
or a star that you are unable to touch
once you get started on your journey.
May you remember all
  you have had from the start
and all that is yours forever.

— Mary Klock Labdon

Dreams Come True
One Step at a Time

When going through life
and traveling in the direction
of your dreams, the best way
to get ahead is the simplest way:

Take it one step at a time.

Don't look over your shoulder; if you do,
you'll feel the weight of all your
yesterdays upon you.
And don't worry about what lies ahead.
By the time you get to
the bend in the road
or the crest of the hill,
you're going to be better and stronger
than you ever were before.

Just go a step at a time,
one day at a time.
And you'll find a rich, thankful life
you never thought you could afford.

— A. Rogers

Promise Yourself

*P*romise yourself that you'll always remember what a special person you are ← Promise yourself that you'll hold on to your hopes and reach out for your stars ← Promise yourself that you'll live with happiness over the years and over the miles ← Promise yourself that you'll "remember when..." and you'll always "look forward to..." ← Promise yourself that you'll do the things you have always wanted to do ← Promise yourself that you'll cherish your dreams as treasures you have kept ← Promise yourself that you'll enjoy life day by day and step by step ← Promise yourself a life of love and joy and all your dreams come true.

— Collin McCarty

Don't Ever Forget That
You Are Special

*D*on't ever forget that you are unique.
Be your best self
and not an imitation of someone else.
Find your strengths
and use them in a positive way.
Don't listen to those
who ridicule the choices you make.
Travel the road that you have chosen
and don't look back with regret.
You have to take chances
to make your dreams happen.
Remember that there is plenty of time
to travel another road — and still another —
in your journey through life.
Take the time to find the route
that is right for you.

*You will learn something valuable
from every trip you take,
so don't be afraid to make mistakes.
Tell yourself that you're okay
just the way you are.
Make friends who respect your true self.
Take the time to be alone, too,
so you can know just how terrific
your own company can be.
Remember that being alone
doesn't always mean being lonely;
it can be a beautiful experience
of finding your creativity,
your heartfelt feelings,
and the calm and quiet peace deep inside you.
Don't ever forget that you are special.*

— *Jacqueline Schiff*

Follow Your Destiny,
Wherever It Leads You

*T*here comes a time in your life when you realize that if you stand still, you will remain at this point forever. You realize that if you fall and stay down, life will pass you by.

Life's circumstances are not always what you might wish them to be. The pattern of life does not necessarily go as you plan. Beyond any understanding, you may at times be led in different directions that you never imagined, dreamed, or designed. Yet if you had never put any effort into choosing a path, or tried to carry out your dream, then perhaps you would have no direction at all.

Rather than wondering about or questioning the direction your life has taken, accept the fact that there is a path before you now. Shake off the "why's" and "what if's," and rid yourself of confusion. Whatever was — is in the past. Whatever is — is what's important. The past is a brief reflection. The future is yet to be realized. Today is here.

Walk your path one step at a time — with courage, faith, and determination. Keep your head up, and cast your dreams to the stars. Soon your steps will become firm and your footing will be solid again. A path that you never imagined will become the most comfortable direction you could have ever hoped to follow.

Keep your belief in yourself and walk into your new journey. You will find it magnificent, spectacular, and beyond your wildest imaginings.

— Vicki Silvers

ACKNOWLEDGMENTS

The following is a partial list of authors whom the publisher especially wishes to thank for permission to reprint their works.

PrimaDonna Entertainment Corp. for "Trust in Yourself" by Donna Fargo. Copyright © 1997 by PrimaDonna Entertainment Corp. All rights reserved. Reprinted by permission.

Barbara J. Hall for "The Power of Change Is in Your Hands" and "Only You Can Make the Right Things Happen in Your Life." Copyright © 1997 by Barbara J. Hall. All rights reserved. Reprinted by permission.

Dena Dilaconi for "Create Your Own World." Copyright © 1997 by Dena Dilaconi. All rights reserved. Reprinted by permission.

Regina Hill for "The Secret to Life Is Living It One Day at a Time." Copyright © 1997 by Regina Hill. All rights reserved. Reprinted by permission.

Jancarl Campi for "Never Let Go of Hope." Copyright © 1997 by Jancarl Campi. All rights reserved. Reprinted by permission.

Donna Newman for "Just Be Yourself." Copyright © 1997 by Donna Newman. All rights reserved. Reprinted by permission.

Jennifer Eller for "Never Let Go of the Dreams in Your Heart." Copyright © 1997 by Jennifer Eller. All rights reserved. Reprinted by permission.

Pamela Owens Renfro for "Be Strong and Don't Give Up." Copyright © 1997 by Pamela Owens Renfro. All rights reserved. Reprinted by permission.

Debra McCleary for "To Get What You Want Out of Life...." Copyright © 1997 by Debra McCleary. All rights reserved. Reprinted by permission.

Michelle Richards for "Success Has No Limits...." Copyright © 1997 by Michelle Richards. All rights reserved. Reprinted by permission.

Nancye Sims for "Let Your Heart Show You the Way" and "Do Whatever You Need to Do...." Copyright © 1997 by Nancye Sims. All rights reserved. Reprinted by permission.

Anne Larnella Hood for "When You're Struggling Over a Difficult Decision...." Copyright © 1997 by Anne Larnella Hood. All rights reserved. Reprinted by permission.

Stephanie Robinson for "A Creed for Being the Best You Can Be." Copyright © 1997 by Stephanie Robinson. All rights reserved. Reprinted by permission.

Caroline Kent for "Live Your Life with Courage." Copyright © 1997 by Caroline Kent. All rights reserved. Reprinted by permission.

Lisa Marie Yost for "There Is Only One Key to Success: Never Quit!" Copyright © 1997 by Lisa Marie Yost. All rights reserved. Reprinted by permission.

Vickie M. Worsham for "You Can Design Your Own Destiny." Copyright © 1997 by Vickie M. Worsham. All rights reserved. Reprinted by permission.

A careful effort has been made to trace the ownership of poems used in this anthology in order to obtain permission to reprint copyrighted materials and give proper credit to the copyright owners. If any error or omission has occurred, it is completely inadvertent, and we would like to make corrections in future editions provided that written notification is made to the publisher:

BLUE MOUNTAIN PRESS, INC., P.O. Box 4549, Boulder, Colorado 80306.